The Bible of the Beasts of the Little Field

by Susan Fromberg Schaeffer

FICTION

FALLING

ANYA

TIME IN ITS FLIGHT

THE QUEEN OF EGYPT

POETRY

THE WITCH AND THE WEATHER REPORT

GRANITE LADY

RHYMES AND RUNES OF THE TOAD

ALPHABET FOR THE LOST YEARS

The Bible of the Beasts of the Little Field

POEMS BY
SUSAN FROMBERG SCHAEFFER

E. P. Dutton
New York

For Neil and T. Georgics

ACKNOWLEDGMENTS

Some of the poems in this volume first appeared in the following magazines, to whose editors grateful acknowledgment is made: *Centennial Review, Chelsea, Chicago Review, College English, Concerning Poetry, Croton Review, Dakota Territory, Denver Quarterly, Fiddlehead, Gallimaufry, Little Magazine, The Midwest Quarterly, Minnesota Review, Ms., Ohio Journal, Salmagundi, Stonecloud.*

Contents

I. REST

Rest

This is when the bones
Sleep inside the body

Like sleek white lemurs
And the smooth green pastures

Have finished
And the sun has set in its cave

And the strange
Hibernation begins and begins.

The skull, chalk steeple,
Is lined with black bats, sleeping,

And the gold bells,
Muffled with canvas.

There will be no news,
Good or bad,

For there is no one to hear it.
There is no such thing

As mail, or pyramids, or sphinxes,
But there are many mummies.

And in all the rooms,
Small clocks crumbling to dust.

Time is passing, and not.
Old chimes settle everywhere, thickly.

The gophers carpet their holes,
Fold their paws, and dream on.

On the pillow,
A fan of dark hair

Opens itself;
It is a dark sky,

And will not brighten.
Some grieve so over this:

The long pause
Before it begins.

New Light

1.

A simple enough affair;
Only turning off the light
And the trees rushed in

Like guests left waiting in ball gowns
At the door,
Too long shivering in the cold,

And the stars, attended by loud winds;
There was a difference in them,
The way they kept their place,

From here, seeming no more than steel nails,
Cheap,
Showing through the blue,
Hasty, crude,

A sloppy job, this canvas tent
We trust ourselves to night by night,
Accepting it as inevitable,
That deep dark,

While out beyond its walls,
Wild beasts prowl,
Their tails atwitch with rage

And we, no longer afraid.

2.

Where did the wonder go?
That sudden blink in the fabric
Of a tiny stage throwing open wide its doors,

And the drama so easy to write down,
The puppets growing their sorrows on their strings,
The lightning sketched on, the smiling moon,
The loon circling the lake,
The ripples spreading out in silver curves,

Either puppet or puppeteer,
The strings vanishing, until they tightened
Like rings on limbs swollen
From the heat and cold,

Too many seasons.

3.

Of course, doors still open
Although one does not
Necessarily hurry to describe the scene,
And one does not enter the same way,

That miniature version of self
Hung high on the walls, nestled in the angle
Where they join,

Which sat, legs crossed,
Smoking a cigarette,
Tapping ashes into air,
Having long ago slid down a beam

And settled, sound asleep, behind our eyes,
Measuring its dreams meticulously,
Poisonous drop by drop into our tears,

And now, waking from a dream
It seems so easy to say
It was a dream, falling back asleep,
Framing them in the Persian blues
And golds of night,

And this new, fatal love
Of the gleamless dark.

4.
Somewhere, of course,
There is a strange sun
Attended by a few faithful clouds,

The moon having long ago gone off,
Where the music is only
Of dry leaves blowing upon hard rock,
And marble statues wed
In a clatter of shells

And a beach without sand
Of valuable waves and priceless,
Unreachable white dunes.

5.
Shall I say
We no longer care who goes under,
What angel is washed up on the shore?

Then believe that I lie
And that the sun opens up its doors
Letting the white butterflies
Flutter and fall into the hair

Of young girls, and the young men
Are struck completely dumb,
And on dark days, flights of dark moths,
A black halo for the sun

In the shattering sky
And the only sound
Is the sound of chimes

And daily, new people
Walk out of the waves,
Shaking the foam from their thick hair

In visions of green rock and fish,
Their eyes open, and yet not,

And the world shall never end,
However often the sun shall flicker
And go dark.

Confession in April

Dear Lord, I have sinned against thee.
For I do not love all flowers equally.

For daffodils have come up in my yard instead of tulips.
For I hate their stupid yellow faces

And say they are no better than weeds.
For I have turned spiteful,

And admire the cats who do bite through their necks.
For I finger my calluses from the planting,

And resent them still further.
For I blame them for their nature.

Yet once planted, they could but be what they are.
For I resent the earth that they eat in their growing.

For even the crow who devoured a nestling before me
Is more approved in my sight.

For I will not accept them, and say, "I cannot."
For if I had courage

I would root them up by their heads
And leave them as carcass.

For my anger is implacable against them.
Yet they grow in clusters like families

And still are detestable.
For I say, "How could this happen?"

As if it counted to measure.
For I tell myself I loved the barrenness better.

For I act as if this were the last year,
And encourage the winds against them

And hate the rains which suckle them up.
For I walk neither to the right nor left.

But would trample upon them.
For in the morning I wish it were evening

So they would be gone from my sight.
For I cannot forgive.

For all day my face is pressed against the glass
And my eye is evil.

For I eye my neighbor's hose and will it to burst
And drown them entirely. For they seem so proud.

For they have spent the winter feeling worms
At their white skins, and have not complained to the air.

They do not cry out, "We are cold,"
Though the wind blows against rawly,

Or against heat when the sun bakes down upon them.
For they are not really ugly.

For much can be said to assert them,
Yet they anger me beyond all sanity.

For I suspect their connivance against my favorite tulips.
For their golds are gall to me.

For in truth, my will is not done.

The Moles

Twitchell Cemetery, Vermont

God only knows what we were doing there,
Visiting Freddie, so long dead,
In that place of stopped hearts,

As if he were ours, ours only,
Died 1818, age four years, nine months;

Perhaps it was merely his stone,
Perhaps it was not Freddie at all,
But his father, younger than we were,

That day, that year, 1818,
Who carved the little lamb
Stroke by stroke out of found marble

Until he fashioned a shape for his own heart,
Until he felt each stroke of his blade.
Not as sentimental as we had first thought,

A lamb, not a puppy, not the child's pet,
Meaning, as did the stone of his sister,
Gone home.

Oh, it was a strange day,
As if black birds were stirring the air to storm
Everywhere,

The cold, white clouds, the stunning blue sky,
And the mountains rising, stone over stone,

The stones in the midst of that greenery
Signaling winter,
Its endless, separating snows,

Making those drifts seem, for the moment,
Tame, nothing fearful. Never before
Did we so feel our helplessness in the face of enormity,

Shrunk to this little lamb
Who gazed at us out of his black eye, over his shoulder,
While the black mold mottled his back,

And the picturesque stones tilting this way and that,
A forgotten town all askew,
And we were naïve

To lean so on his sister,
Poor Emmeline,
Who died in the second summer,

And her stone fell straight back,
The crown piece flying farthest,
One stone in three pieces.

What a horror, as if a god had fallen,
And how fast we jumped
To put up that heavy marble,

One pin holding the big slab,
Like the pin in a hip of a soldier,
The other, two plates in the head of a skull.

Poor Emmeline, we said then,
She never had luck.

It was then that we noticed the feel of the ground,
And the dates of the parents
Who lived thirty-six years after Freddie,

Waiting ten for Emmeline,
And when she was gone, no foolish carving
For that spongy ground,

That ground that seemed so ready to let the boot through
To the dead that we walked on.

It did not feel right, walking on the dead,
And then it did, as if this were the earth's crust,
And now, given up all disguises.

We kept telling ourselves they were down deep
But after the fall of that stone, it was hard to believe it,

When we realized, it was only moles,
Little moles, hundreds of them,
Tunneling the loam, creating this terror our boots

Would go through to poor Emmeline and poor Freddie,
Those sleek moles, opposers of gardens,
And we thought, as we left, or thought we left,

Through the white wicket,
This was the wrong garden for them,
The fruits were too deep for their paws and their noses,

But the lamb's black eye caught us,
And as if we could read the mole notes,
We knew those furry, destroying angels,
Their sharp teeth and their earth song,
Their deep mission and worm tunnels;

And though little Freddie haunted our sleep
Like one of the quickest,
We knew then we would always be wrong.

Scene

The cow is black and white,
The rest
Of the scene is familiar.

The grass,
The glass sky,

The peace that bubbles up
From the many mouths
Of the ground,

Several white steeples,
A rose growing rampant,
The fort, forgotten,
Access gone,

All edges
Sharp as thin tin:

It cuts the eye
Not threatening blindness,
But promising.

The routine kind
Where the hills blue,
The mountains gray,
The sky fades,

The greens swell the leaves
As if a storm were coming;

Easy to imagine the spatter
Of rain,
The crack of thunder,
The sky shattering, old glass,

And it will do all these things,
And it is only one night

Amidst the innumerable.

Nebraska

The simple land,
Flat as the palm of God's hand,
Cows crunch; laundry flaps in the yard.
The grass paints itself green;
"See how easy, how easy."
The calf is fitted under the stomach
Of his mother,
A neat little block.
Two horses, eye to eye,
Tails swishing like tassels
Of Victorian fans,
The two bright blue flies.

The pines point up,
The sky calm as the eye of a cow,
The tiny hospital
The size of a house,
The church across the road, much bigger.
Patients are checking out
Of the windows of one
And into the other.
They are climbing the branches
Of pine trees like ladders.
In the morning, you can see them,
Fleecy spirits of mist.

The glistening twigs of trees,
The leaves turning, like little angels,
From God.
Outside the church, Christ
Is driftwood and dimensional,
Imploring, stretching his hands.

Under his cold toe,
The young thing waits at the corner
For someone, folds her arms
On her breast,
Her left foot keeps tapping.

The last of the bats
Are falling asleep
In the homes' gothic turrets.
The paint keeps on peeling,
Hanging on like ragged moths.

The pines are imploring the wind,
"One moment, one moment."
In single file, the cows,
Good pedestrians,
Are heading for home.

II. THERE WAS A TIME

There Was a Time

There was a time
When certainties fell on us
Like gold,

When it was always clear weather.
We turned trees to etched glass.

We never noticed,
Or else it didn't matter
That no breeze passed
Through rooms like a bird,

That not one tree or leaf
Could be seen, or heard,
In full summer.

The world around us
Was gold only,
And this seemed good.

Then our fingers clattered
Like metal on metal

And then we understood.

The Book of Hours

I.
This is the book of hours of busyness.
Yet, before I begin,

Twelve months in a year seems too little,
And twenty-four hours in a day

Seems such a great space,
So many to go through,

As in a country full of states.
And there are days

Which drag themselves
From hour to hour

Like the manacled criminal
Behind the stone

While others
Fly by so fast

The air fills with bats
And the churches toll out their hearts
In a conflagration of bells.

II.
The quiet hours are gilt-edged
Like clouds,
At sunrise or sunset.

Whether they move, or don't move,
Whether they are gray and heavy and full of rain,
Or empty,

Going like smoke,
At their edges they are golden.

Today I saw an empty blue sky
Filling with clouds, rolling in,
Wave after wave,

More slowly and more stately
Than the planets traveling their arcs.
And then the day

Closed over my head.
There was a quick vision
Of thick trees from wide windows,

Gilded by autumn,
Mimicking the spring, its chartreuses,

And the touch of the air on my skin
Was cold.
It was spring under ice.

III.
Did I say I like the thinning clouds most?
And that city graveyards
Resemble small cities,

Small skylines against large,
The angels on the roofs of the small houses,
Up for a glimpse of the sky,

While country burying grounds
Are empty and quiet,
And come on in surprising places,

At the end of a pasture,
Visited by a cow or a pig,
And there is always

The chatter of squirrels,
And the inhabitants,
With their stone pillows over their faces,

Can make themselves heard.
They go together so nicely
In that plain, shadowed green parlor,

Where the ground sows its own flowers
And plants its own grasses.
Privacy. Sunsets, sunrises, glass trees in winter.

The unexpected, the unexpected forever.
And under the ground,
Blood speaks to blood.

I have no right to hope for it.

IV.
The night prepares its blue hours,
And its white, iced, changeable moon.

In his room,
The child takes on the same colors.
At these strange hours

After he wakes and sleeps,
The silence is thick as velvet,
The air is luxurious,

There is time to feel
The boards of the floor on one's back,
And also, listen to the dry leaves

Rustle.
These hours are stolen, and fragile,
As when one walks down a lane

In the woods
And comes on a pasture
Spread out like a pocket of silver,

And the cracked moon breaks,
Or goes under.
It is nice

To turn out the lights
And watch shadows only,
Your body

A stringed instrument
Their fingers play upon softly.
A time for music,

And the music rises
Against the dark hours.

V.
From the back window
The new leaves show red.
The hands of the clock move without remorse

Or sorrow toward a new day.
You cheat, pick up your clippers,
Throw on a coat,

And live like a plant with the plants.
Well, then the pipe bursts,
And the ceiling rains down brown water,

The inside cats clamor,
They want their dinner,
The outside cats scratch at the screen door.

Is there an inch
Without living creatures?

There is the Japanese chime
Of a storm window breaking
Just as the storm breaks,

There are no voices
At the other end of the wire,
Or what they have to say is unpleasant,

The pigeons are cooing their heads off,
Strutting safe in their enamel breastplates,
Piles of letters wait like cold, dirty dishes:

Why don't you write me?
Why don't you ever call me?
Who ate the last piece of bread

And what shall we do now?

My skirt
Is constantly weighted with small hands;
No wonder the hems give.

Who has checked on visiting hours?
I suppose this problem is real,
And major,

Lamb chops or veal.
Everyone hangs so on the decision.

And the paint will not
Come off the old door.
It looks like a bad case

Of the plague.
There is no going back now.
We have to finish it,

Fall, Winter, Summer, Spring.
This is so ordinary.
How did we find it,

This perfect door to go through,
To that thing, so peculiar,
The ordinary life.

The Living

The early light falls in peacefully,
Playing no favorites,

On all the things which exist,
And all I have willed to exist,

And frankly, I am at a loss
To say which category claims me,

For I have seen the sun
Turn in the sky like a grindstone,

And the blue dust settle as air,
And I have willed myself to existence

So many times,
I would say of it, habit,

Yet it is not automatic,
And always, is painful.

For the statues, and the baskets,
And the doll,
And the domed radio and the glove boxes,

The silk roses, the sampler,
Breathe in and out, as I do at this hour,

Or is it only this hour,
These strange tricks of the light,

Which is not yet quite light,
But confuses, and outside,

The brick houses stir
And are rose-colored, beat with blood

As I do,
And try to stand against storms.

For my clocks tick as the hearts of birds.
For my tulips speak to the carpets.
For they close, like sleep,
Having seen enough, and more than enough.

For today, all the creatures
Which have done the creating
Visit like relatives. For my room
Fills with forests, cherry trees,

Mahogany, oaks,
And they move through each other like breezes.
For the sheep are here to honor their wool,
And the silkworm in his tent

No more amazed than the elephant
Who sends only his eye to peer at small wares.

For today, my doll and I understand one another,
And the motto of my sampler
Sustains me entirely.

For today is the seventh day,
And the clock and the heart lie down together,
And find no differences.

And my ancestors move about in their full skirts,
Their kerchiefs, their dark suits,

Hands over mouths,
Then touching everything as if it were hot.

For they pause before me and nod their approval.
And today, all the things I have made
Chime their hearts out in peals of small, silvery bells.

For I have continued existing.

There Was Something

There was something I wanted to say
About the weather.
That it was divine? Something like that.

That it was the supreme being,
The breath behind all things? Yes.
And in them.

Nothing so simple
As a long line of dromedaries
Across the bone-white rim of cresting sands,

The bedouins white, the Lazari,
The whole scene rippling, the hint,
Yes, this is painted, on cellophane,

See how it crinkles—

But the complex, as when one asks,
"Will it rain?" As when one dials, "Will it rain?"
"Hot enough for you, hot enough for you, hot enough?"
Ask the possessed, not speaking with their own tongues,

The gasoline devils, oh they burn.
And the prophets of bones
Who answer, there are no clouds,

The air is dry (even feeling it
Between fingers, like fabric),
But the bones sing Mass to the body,

They bend the knees down,
They bend down the back,
The bone moans in its socket

Under the small hills which cry,
We are lent you as crutches,
Your spine is a ladder,

You can climb it,
Above the clouds there is no weather.

What are your hands?

Spread them, veins in a leaf,
And the potter's vessel, the skull,
With its many round doorways,

In my father's skull are many mansions;
So says the mouse as he goes in and out.
The crops blacken in spite of us.

The crops push past their fences.
The pumpkins shrivel, the pumpkins burst.
Only the sky tills its fields, reaps clouds.

"Today it was so hot," she said,
"I thought I would melt into grease.
We shall have no potatoes."

"It has proven hot here in Kansas," he wrote,
"The dust blows in like furies.
I doubt we will get hold on this land."

"I want to mix the sun and the rain as my father,
The apothecary," she wrote;
The next week she died of the fever.

The weather is pure, sing the bones.
We whiten to angels, we whiten.
There are impurities called lives;

We do recognize them;
They thicken the weather.
Yet, in its mercy, it stays.

In the beginning, in a moment of thoughtlessness
It made its pact with a rib.
The rib has whitened to the glare

Of one thousand suns;
They wear the white robes of judges
And no flesh may approach them.

As they recede and recede to that point
Out of vision,
Sing bone, sing brother, sing harp of the ribs,

Sing ankle, sing elbow,
To dirge down the flesh.

The Windows

The morning light sanctifies all the terrible objects,
The knives, the serviceable dishes,

Which return in their tiny orbits again and again
Like used moons,

And also the strange silence of this one hour before creation;
And my own breath is not human

But is a breeze through the winds and the rushes
And my bones are not yet,

There is no human element,
The human element is not yet,

But green saplings, saying what soon will be
And the yard has gathered time to itself in its greenery.

The trees dance, the wind blows,
Bluejays drink of the cracked fountain,

The sun opens, petal by petal,
And the clouds move in their silence,

They fly in flocks like white geese;
They are intelligent.

Little waters puddle and splash,
Sing, see the flood has pulled back,

There is a sighing that compasses everything,
Yes, it even rests on four pillars,

And the willow bends its hair to the blowing
And the sky's ancient silks billow in blueness, up and again.

Now the flowers do speak one to the other
And even bend down to the little worm

Who goes so hard through his tunnel,
With joy they open their mouths to the tigery bee.

This is before, before everything,
Yes it is true an angel stands at the gate;

Although there is no gate, yet there is one indeed.
Oh this is before, and all is still then

But my heart crawls with time, fills with it like burrowing
      ants;
To them, I am only more earth.

In a pointy white tower, a steeple, a petal splash of pealings,
A blazing forth of the sun, a throat cry,

The ivy becomes ivy, my hands become my hands,
The cat crosses the yard; she has divided,

Her eyes full of purpose;
And in the high tower, I see the round face with its numbers,

Veined marble and iron,
So the air fills with tickings,

So my blood ticks,
So the rooms now tick to their purpose,

Thus the hands of the clock are the flaming swords of angels,
So this little time comes to its close.

The Book of Fear

This is The Book of Hours of Fear,
Of fear of the hours, the days,

The months and the years,
Identical as boxes, small ones or great ones,

So little difference they can be named
By a number, any one a twin to the other,

Fear of the great leafing elms,
Each resembling the other.

Pick the one that is yours, the King ordered,
And the human eye could not decide.

And then came the one with a difference,
And it bent somewhat,

And its leaves were strange color.
It was dying, and so it stood out.

The hours of people who are certainly different,
Who pursue their grave and gracious grails, separate,

Who feel their uniqueness burn in like a fever,
And yet, I say they resemble; I say they fit in.

Something like a uniformed army obeying one general,
They all storm the castle, be it kettle or pot,

Or this year, chrome, skirt and child.
Yes, they do differ, everyone agrees on it,

Yet they fit in; they fit.
So I submit this grave truth:

In nature, no two things resemble,
Except all creation (a minor cavil)

And nature is a bore, tirelessly repeating
The same song with small variations,

And someone heard it, and thereafter,
He lived with one ear.

This is the hour of fear, when the touch
Of the head on the pillow jars the skull's

Huge halls and theaters, and when the lids shut on night,
The footlights start in with their burning,

The actresses and actors skillful with make-up,
And in nightmares, small figures, black-cloaked,

Try nailing the door shut.
But this is routine, this is expected.

And the actors make their motions
Which compel with their magic

Which cannot be resisted. And they demand
"Give us our lines." It is seen they wear

Striped suits with numbers.
They are murderers and assassins.

Will you accept your destiny, your bride?
The King asked the Lion.

Will you rest your head on her breast?
Not this one, said the Lion.

For her dowry is the pain of the sharp sun above her.
See how it gleams on her cleaver.

That smile, meaning off with the head,
And my whole body stiffens with fear of creation,

And draws away from it, as if from torch-fire.
Will you accept this? asked the King,

For I might as well tell you, your choices are gone,
You shall lie down with her,

For it is written, the lion shall lie down with the scythe.
You are coming to love her already.

Who else shines so in smiling;
Though she is sharp, she never will cut you,

Except you forget this, never to leave her.
But what of my child, whose skin burns like hot metal,

Whose throat chokes on a bone,
And my husband, who looks in room after room,

(For this is only one life among many)
And this destiny, I did not choose it.

When it bit like a serpent,
I stared at the sun, its tail hot and brazen,

Yet I was not cured. It would not cure me.
And when I closed my eyes, the air filled with notes of strange
    music

Which I knew formed the answers,
But I could not read them.

Pity of self, whispers the grass, the ancient affliction.
There is no remedy for it.

And in the twenty-fourth hour of fear,
The sun struck twelve times, and all was accomplished.

And the army marched on the castle,
And the Lion lay down on the knife. As had been predicted,

He was learning to love it,
And the identical trees and the flowers and the grasses

And the birds and the clouds sung in chorus,
"All is accomplished, all is accomplished."

The Months and Their Phases

A woman stands
In a foreign land,
She is familiar;

Her back
Presses against the arch.
Its frame is white,
And her dress falls white against it.

The balcony falls away into darkness
As if it never existed,
And so, too, the glass doors,
Opening out, swallowed.

Will he come,
The man bearing clouds in his arms,
Or was she wrong all this long time?

Was it her mother,
Her arms full of hydrangeas,
Blue-cloud blossoms,

Or did she herself bring them?
It has been such a long while.
The green sky floods in,

The brass ages.

This is before the rain,
But after,
Much occurs, so much.

How accidentally and perfectly
The lime of her shawl and the lime of her glass
Bleed into the air, complementing.

She remembers now his cheeks were pure gold,
As was his helmet.
And she notes, absently,
The sea has learned silences.

What has the castle to do
With the peasants
As they stoop in the fields
Gathering turnips?

A clean-aproned woman
With stomach of pumpkin,
Pushes back the hot wings of her kerchief.

Oxen make ready to offer their cartloads
Of grain,
And the sentry stands watching,
As does one pig, and two horses.

A horse comes from the barrier
On a mission most urgent.
Above, Jove drives his farm chariot
Through the dangerous sky,
Holding his lantern.

She notes
All light is pure gold.
The towers are so high below him
They rise into the sky,

Rocks in the shallows.
Sensibly, he has taken precautions.
His dray horses sprout wings
Of cheap metal.

Where is the man with his arms full of clouds?
Something sounds,
A trumpet or thunder.
Fish swim, and go deeper.

Snow everywhere.
She shivers, draws her shawl tighter.
The women in the hut
Have done with their washing.
They sit,
Skirts raised over their knees.

The little sheep huddle.
The beehives sport peaked roofs of snow.
The men chop at the bare trees.
A donkey begins his ascent,
Strapped with bundles of faggots.

In the snow,
The castle is so far off
It seems an illusion, unnecessary.
The birds will peck for their food.

Outside, someone stomps toward the woman,
Her shawl over her mouth and her nose.
Her little cloud-breaths
Rise up to the others.

A banquet inside the castle.
Few of the animals are real,
Although most are encrusted with gems.
The King, as usual, glowers.
The horses have ridden into the scene,

Or it may only seem so.
The parade of knights and banners
Is a war in dead earnest.
The banquet continues.

It is always the long table,
The rows of horses, of helmets,
And some fool who stops what is expected
To fondle the dog.

Perhaps it was not true, the lake full of fire.
To the women in the field,
The castle is only a border.

They gather the hay into gold hives.
The men belt up their robes,
Suffering with hot scythes.
It is as if the castle is sinking.
Only the cathedral's lacy towers and arches
Draw the eye toward it.

Is it going under,
Or is it only a trick of the eye?
She sighs.
It makes no difference.
It is certainly sultry.

Today, the castle is something to flee from.
It seems grayed with age,
Sooty.

The lords and the ladies
Have taken to their horses
Which pace slow and formal
Under trimmings of scarlet
And deep blues of cobalt.

They bleach the day
With their brilliant pet birds.
Behind them, the work always continues.

Before them, the river seems gray,
The peasants who plunge into its waters,
Gray corpses, strange fish.

They are not to be noticed,
Drowned as they seem,
Genitals floating.
Dull, the wheat gathers in sheaves.

All this has happened in a matter of seconds,
Yes she sees it over and over.
Where is the man with his arms full of clouds?
She shudders.

His arms are laden down with them,
But the rest are following,
Stampeding like terrified sheep.

The reliable man in the sky,
Hugging his lantern,
Lets it go out.

The Bible of the Beasts
of the Little Field

1.

I was born unacquainted, the beasts say,
I was born unacquainted,
Everything that creeps, and flies through the firmament,
And swims the deep places,

And they say unto us,
Who is to say that our breaths go down,
And yours go up, and we are struck dumb,

Saying, I know you not, I do not know you,
We have become unacquainted.

2.

Let me number in this new yard as I can:
A multitude of cats, both little and large,
Both one color and brindled, some friendly, some not,
Some lame, some strong-legged,

And birds of many descriptions,
Some red on the head, others on the chest,
Little brown ones, numerous as the seeds they do eat,
A hammerer at wood,

Two strolling pigeons with breastplates of Persian enamel,
Who feel no fear, who walk about my toes,
Who in the morning call to each other
With the thick sound of water
Gushing from all the deep places,

And one red cardinal, and also two bluejays.

3.
Let us consider the animals in the spring.
The Abyssinian mistress has brought forth three black kittens.
In numberless leaves, they number three.
Their nest is an old car, its pipes are their toys.

They will not know us, though we bring milk forth to them.
They stare at us seriously out of blue-button eyes.
How the mighty have fallen!
No, says the cat, I am Ruth, amidst alien corn

And I have multiplied after my kind.
Black queen, my queen.

4.
Is there no end to the humans and all their fenced cities?
Who tend to their vines
And the green blood touches their hands
And now they want red?

The man in the house after is a reproach and a lament.
As they pass by, people hiss at him,
Yet he is innocently clipping his vines.
There was a man who took bricks and threw them.

This is the man.
For he has taken a cat, and broken its back.
For it has crawled to its dying into the yard of the priest.
And what shall be his punishment?

For he has set a trap and caught the cat called Nameless,
And Nameless is crippled.
And what shall his punishment be?
For we have fed Nameless and tried to minister.

For there is much to this matter, as a tree with two leaves
May spread its roots through the yard.
For we must consider Nameless, the cat who was crippled.

5.
Angel with four faces, one of man, one of lion, one ox, one
    eagle,
Come down, come down, angel with four wings,
Always going straight as you gaze,
Resting on your two rings,

One moving you forward, one turning,
And each ring full of eyes,
(For the spirit of the angel rests in the wheels)
Can you inspire such wonder as Nameless?

For Nameless is my savior; he has caused me to green into life,
As a dry root in water, as a wire into its current,
As each green leaf to the sun,
To turn from my winter, to come forth green and golden,

My earth full of petals,
My branches heavy with leaves.

6.
Wherefore did this cat say, Yea, I shall live?
His skin hung on him; his bones showed through him
Like lathing of a dwelling that hath not yet been plastered.
White was his fur with considerable gray patches.

A map of despair is he,
So said we of him as he went his way by us.
He walked in pure pain as a tree that catches on fire.
Up the fence of pain he went, his injured leg with him,
And down again, into the yard.

So he slept before the priest. So he slept before me.
By lifting their heads, others could scare him off milk.
He lay in the greens, and the rain brought him mud-splattered.
Heavy was the air, and the flying bugs crowned him

As if he had died there.
He left, and the earth turned to iron.
He came again, and the earth turned to gold.
Fat and happy was the cat!

For Missy the cat has given him her protection.
For he has given her kittens.
For his fourth foot rests on the ground, and almost will bear
    him.
For he has dug through the wall called despair

And has seen the green sea.
For he has let me press my eye to it,
Although he constantly hisses.
For he has let me touch his head, which was the head of a
    savage.

On that day I was anointed.
On that day I had faith.

7.
Under the sun
I sat on the earth and considered.
I considered the little hill in its baldness.
I considered the little seeds in their pouches

And how the two should be joined.
And as I sat, the sky was blue and the earth was chocolate.
So I took up my trowel, and on the earth's first turning
Discovered a worm.

And the worm was not unusual, no, he was as wide as my finger,
And his color was a dull pink, as the inner part of a body,
And although he was startled, under my eye,
He made his way along the little hill,

And I wondered that I did not fear him,
Or feel disgust at him, but thought I could even see on his body

The head which made the rest ripple after,
As if it were a living wave,

And thought how he went down deep into the cold earth
Making all his apartments, learning the road-marks of pebbles,
And how the sun did not shine for him, or the moon,
Yet still he comes up in tribute to see them

And then makes his bed in the absolute dark.
And I thought then of the flowers,
And how they bore living, one short season nodding
In the pleasant rains and sun showers,

Then fisting back to bulbs for ten months of dreams.
Ten months of dreams! So long for dreams!
No wonder their timbrels and psalteries and little bells
Play so in the yard

And their music starts the season to ticking,
Nor does the worm harm them. Ten months of dreams!
When they come they are emptied out of them;
Their sight is as the clear glass,

They see what is here.
And I saw them and envied.
And the little worm made his way from me.

8.
Lord, the great tree has cast a squirrel down before me,
And the neighbors all say, take him up and make him to eat
For he is only a baby. He lies in this box as he lay on the
        ground,
Arms spread out as if flying, and little legs also,

And his eyes do not wink, but stare only.
Though the wind ruffles the fur of his comely gray tail,
He is dead. Yet I have put
Sugared milk on his lips, for he might yet wake in his box,

And if it were down deep, the worm's will would fail him,
The baby's sky darken, and I could never explain.
He is dead, he is dead, says the weather.
My light does not make his eye to blink, says the sun, nor to
    water,
Nor does the wind do ought but stir him.

Through his small nose comes no little breeze of his own.
The small children think he is sleeping.
Goodnight, goodnight, they say under the trees.
He fell and took up his pose.

He took up his pose and he died.

Yet we have Nameless.
Shall I destroy Nineveh, that great city,
Said the Lord, wherein the people do not know their left hand
From their right hand, and also much cattle?

And also my Nameless?
And also my Nameless?

III. THE FROG POND

Love

Why is love so difficult?
At the very word the heart

Surrounds itself with briars;
But the thorns
Have their own secrets;

With tears, his sword
Slashes through. His face is gashed,
His clothes cut to pieces.

When he finds her,
His tears and his blood
Varnish her face.

He is already
Full of joys and resentments,
And she is ecstatic,

Though the coffin's glass-smash
Surely upsets her.
Her face is sticky;

She asks for his kerchief.
As he sees it stain,
He does not say what he feels,

Nor does she,
Looking at its tarnishing blood.
As they walk home,

Talking of home,
They know not what they say,
They are so full of plans.

I will bandage the walls with drapes,
And wig the bald windows with ruffledom.
The eyes of the house shall not stare

Like wide-open lids
Stiff and unclosing.
We shall have blinds.

And he says, look,
I have seen these boards
Somewhere before,

And this narrow room.
Someday it will warm.
We can feed those shrill cries,

And mirrors, forbidden us,
Are no loss,
Small faces shall give back our own.

What is that chill wind
But a deep breath?
What is that cough
In the attic?

I know
There are flowers quick in the plaster;
They are drawn to the bodies.

From the minute they slammed the door,
They smelled earth;
They argued with each other like lawyers.

They picked each other's pockets.
Someone always woke in the night
And stole from the room.

The shadows were thick.
Each confided in the moon.
There were the illnesses

And the recriminations,
And that mad lady, Memory,
Locked herself in the guest room.

When they could not get her out,
They fed her under the door.
Strange to say, everything prospered,

Though the cat they fed
Ate the pigeon who fed on their crumbs

And when it was over,
There were others left who cried,
And one patched cat

Who kept returning to the scene of the crime,
Saying, though no one understood,
This was love,
This was happiness,

And I, too,
Between hunting the birds,
And the squirrels,
And the one pigeon remaining,

Take time out to mourn.

The Frog Pond

I.
Forgive me love, for loving down
So deep. In the beginning,

We went down to the frog pond,
Stood in the center, learning
The hoarse voice of love.

Green bodies sped about us
On important missions. Above,
The mountains held the lake

Like a chalice. Something
Drank from it, something enormous.

Around us, trees whispered;
A porcupine hung from the high boughs.
There were no

Mosquitoes and no flies.
We bit into each other.

II.
Next came the sea,
And counting the ribs of our bodies
On the ribs of the sand.

When I heard your heart
Opening and closing, I knew
There was someone always going in and out
Doorways to halls

I did not know, and never would.
I cried all night. You slept somewhere
Deep beneath the waves.
The wind blew our door open.

III.
In Rome, beneath the roof of angels,
We felt the heaviness of our bodies.
For the first time,

We were made of flesh alone.
There was never an updraft
To sail on,

And we were stuck
With our relics of bones.
I would have tried

Gilding the house, gilding you.
We left like creatures
Hurled into the dust.

IV.
Of course, we tried going back.
The mosquitoes bit like snakes.

The frogs were silenced,
And the clouds muffled everything
Like water. Before we slept,

They cleared off,
And the last thing we heard
Was the tiger lilies' sharp cries

As they surrendered, one by one,
Their painful oranges to the night.

Were we too much alike?
In the morning,

My nails were long as sun's rays.
We found only
Each other's husks.

Anniversary Room

1.
Broad daylight
And everyone is sleeping.
The air
Is shining, hanging

In hundreds of Chinese sheets,
Such delicate glass.
I would not be the wind,

Having so much polishing,
Though the air
Chimes exquisitely
And for once, the stunned sun

Is quiet and white.

2.
Start
By remembering the old land,
That desert thronging with people
Who would pause before a sea

Shouting for water,
Who would look into your eyes
Hungry for dew,

Who would follow you home
Although you had none,
Inventing intricate histories
Which proved to you
That spurious nest existed,

And always before
You had opened your door.
Remember how you paused
On corners, watching the streets

Widen to rivers
Trying to find a reason to cross over
And there was never
Anything wrong.

3.
Today, love,
Our window is built of twigs,
Our pane, a sudden panel of ice.
We cannot see out,

Although the shadows are icicles
And the light in here
Is the blue light of cold.

Sounds fly upwards,
Like demented black birds
And there are no words.

News falls on us like snow.
The moon dresses now

In her closet,
Turning shy
Of the sharp eyes of stars.

Tonight, without fear,
She wears long white scarves
Of Isadora,

For the wheels of the earth
Have halted,
And a strange planet
Is coming to court.

Stars are following everywhere.
They are light and cold,
And root everywhere.

The moon showers down more.
One nestles between your eyes,
My Hindu.

Is there one between mine?
I see the new planets
Pulsing like hearts.
I feel this one breathe beneath my feet.

I take this veil happily,
Bride of surprise,
That nothing is new.

4.
There are ships coming closer,
And their warm sails billow.
Clouds, come with me
To the world's kitchen

To the chef of the grass,
The connoisseur of oceanic soups,
The clever confectioner of peaks,
That sad keeper of salts,
Desert maker,

And the shy child dropping white shells
Into unknown deep seas.
To live forever
As if sea songs sang to one's ear.

Carpets fly in the up-drafts;
Angels come here to rest.
Love, melt this window down,
Or we never shall leave.

5.
Something is wrong!
A window of steel and glass,
Yet all the framed people
Jump down to the floor

Dancing old dances,
Refusing all order,
Pulling flowers from the walls,

Their hair full of petals and birds.

The ballerina in the dome
Will not come out.
I am not born, she cries.

And the others
Empty their pockets of time,
Raining it down on her like dust,
Bridal rice.

She creeps to the edge, lies down,
Gasps at the fall to the floor.
And her dress is long.

She feels it lap over her toes
And shivers for joy.

Bells
Peal in the steeple,
And the people line its walls,
Warm bats, upside down.

The moon will not go,
Although the sun turns the corner,
Coming forward, shyly,

The ivy's endless hands
Have joined theirs together,
For already

All walls have turned green.

And I tell you,
There is no knowing
What will happen now.

Jubilate Agno: Thomas Cat

for Christopher Smart and his Geoffrey

For I love my cat with my heart.
For I love my cat beyond all reason.
For he is not even a cat. He is love in his fur.

For he is not even a good cat.
For when he is hungry he rips open the trash bags
And spreads his tins all around

So all may know his hunger and feed him.
For he is willful. For when his box is not changed
He squats on the furniture in threatening posture.

For it is said he has no soul at all and cannot love me
For he has no understanding, yet when I am sick
He lies with me and will not drive off no matter the menace;

For he lies on my chest and puffs his breath into my nose
As if it would help me,
For when I wake in a chill his hot paw rests on my arm

Where it makes a warm circle;
For after surgeries, he finds out the wound and would knead upon
    it
As if driving it out of the body;

For he loves his mother, although it is said he should not,
Yet he goes to her daily for washings;
For he never will swat her, nor will he hiss after,

For he waits for her to eat up her dinner.
For he also waits for his father. For he is not even normal.
For he lies in the sun like a rug and leaps from his sleep

And chases the stairs. For he pops out from chairs without any
    reason;
For he starts into air and claps his front paws together;
For he jumps up the wall and slides down the light with no
    explanation;

For his forehead is wide and has clouds behind it;
For his eyes are so round they are God's perfect circles;
For his cheeks are so puffy they seem to have wings;

For he is the gray color of God's clouds before He thought
    of the sky and the land;
For his eyes are the green color of the sea when God's ships
    are happy;
For his eyes are two stars which can move in the dark;

For he is beautiful, yet he has no vanity and does not pause
    before mirrors
(Yet once he did when he still was a child)
For he sits on the window and taps on the glass

To say boundaries are arbitrary;
For he does not have nine lives but he lives his one well;
For although he will hide from the guests

He will come forth like a soldier to do battle with a bug,
For he knows that I hate them,
For he enters the tunnels of paper bags

And resurrects himself with splits and crackles of fire;
For he jumps straight into the air, disproving gravity;
For he falls on his feet whenever I drop him,

For though he walks away huffily, still he comes back in
    forgiveness.
For his heart beats faster than the heart of a human;
For he uses himself up fast in our service;

For he sits at the window dreaming of birds in his teeth,
Yet he forgives us his captivity.
For he purrs constantly, so we may know he is ticking;

For although he cannot kiss, yet he tries, licking his own lips.
For when he sits upon you and looks on your face, his own
    is quiet and serious;

For he endures the screams of small children,
Which is hard since he is even smaller himself.
For he lies on a green rug like a calf in the field.

For he lies on his back like his old enemy, the dog.
For a white triangle shows itself between his front paws;
For when he is there, you are there with him;

For he always forgives;
For he lives the life that you give him and still walks all
    stately,
For he is loyal to his master, no matter who feeds him,

Yet this is contrary to what is reported,
For he always is cheerful unless he is dying;
For he sleeps in small boxes like Everyman

And does not mind it.
For he is love, and may go in his faith.

IV. EVERYTHING

Seeing Snow

How remarkable, watching
The first thick and drifting snow
Falling this way,

Softly, and with no purpose;
Though purpose will intervene
And put the whitened scene
To use,

Comparing it to all other snows;
The mind, like an unruly dog,
Worrying it;

Remarking on how
I watch the snow today
More as simple snow
Unrelated to myself or mood,

And then, putting it aside
And seizing it again,
Squeezing it for metaphor,

While still, it is true
For one brief instant
All else was gone but snow,

The mind as close
To whiteness
As the white snow
Lying like the softest fur

On all the gaunt, black, free arms,

As when a hollow globe

Is fallen to the floor
And smashed to bits,
And the blank pieces of the inside face up,
Lying about
Like so many
Snow-covered, unprinted antic lawns.

It is that true white moment,
That skipped beat in space
That I now celebrate.

Everything

Oh, the pink geranium clouds
And the two white horses.

A procession of skunks,
Black and white.

White snowballs, cascading.
The trellis' brilliant white lattice.

One gold dome
And two red maples.

Red cliff and blue mountain,
The cat at the side of the road.

Some yellow daisies
And also some white.

The swell of a hill,
The dip of a valley.

A kind coolness,
Patting everything.

Water falling over rock.
The running stream;

The stagnant pool,
Its drowned gray sticks.

Everything is here.
Even the bulldozer, bright yellow.

Even its pocks
Of red rust.

The Arrival

The night the angel arrived,
The King and Queen gave up
Sleeping on their backs.

Their subjects noticed immediately.
Royalty chose the gnomic road.
The air needs no explanation.

When they granted the angel
An audience,
All the tall globes housing
The brides and grooms of wedding cakes
Shattered.

When they granted citizenship,
All the golden-haired children turned silver;
The rest white overnight.

Nights,
The King and Queen took turns;
They kept awake.

The Queen
Thought of the lines in the angel's face,
Of stitching a new tapestry,
Threads the color of storms,

The peaks of the castle under the waves,
Exquisite white coral beneath undulate greens.

She stitched abominations
Into the rooms of the clouds;
Twisting bodies,
A man

Gnarled like a tree,
Taking root next to the throne.

They rode out among the people
Who thought the fuss would end with the weather.
The angel dug potatoes,
Flew the skies, throwing down oranges.
The crows

Brooded the loss of the topmost fruits,
The merchants happy, and fat.

When the angel died,
The King and Queen refused food.
For three days, the Queen
Wove orange threads
In her sleep.
Worst, the little folk in the dolls' houses

Would not move,
The robes stiff to the winds.
When the bells woke the King and Queen,
Tolling and chiming,

They ordered Christmas trees razed,
Caged birds exiled,
And the sextons

To cease winding the churches.
In the hot light,
Steeples flaked to grayness.

They resumed
Sleeping on their backs,
Hands folded on chests,

Stiff in their robes.
They had assumed their kingdom
Held one immortal.

The Angel

The day they buried the angel

Nothing much
Changed in the town;

The sun struck white adobe
Until walls seemed celestial pages,
But it had always been that way;

Poppies rioted,
Begonias spilled their pinks;
The sleek donkeys
Arrived with carts of oranges;

It was some time before they noticed
The sound of the sea
Was missing, its surface

Still as a mirror.
The green fish were not jumping
Out and back in.

The King counseled patience
While the Queen raged at the days,
Commanded her seamstresses
To cut each royal gown in half,

Join one half to another's.

Through it all,
The King kept his dignity,
Until
She smashed the seer's ball of glass

With her shoe,
Stabbed the village idiot
With her tortoise-shell comb.

He tried reasoning;
The wise men came.
She threw them downstairs.
She said she preferred her seashell:

It was wiser;
Even when she rested on her bier,
Making sure of its length,
The shell was pressed to her ear.

The King began to complain,
A woman with a shell for an ear
Was no wife;

People began to remember the strange snow
At the funeral of the angel.
They claimed it had swirled into wings.

When the people
Felt their shoulder blades itch
And she saw the wet feathers sprouting,
She threw down her fan in disgust.

Then she felt her own shoulders
Tingling. When she went to find
The gold box holding her last wish

The King followed,
Taking his also.
They were last seen

Swimming out to sea
And into the sun

Their white wings
Turning to the gray fins of the shark.

Darkness

Prince of Darkness,
You lift your cloak
And all is black, no birds

Sing there.
Everywhere,
There are black flowers
And strange, thin shapes

Who pick them and drift off,
Dark arms full of blossoms.

They rustle like paper
And that is the single sound.

There is no weather,
Just a chill, a dampness,

No paths to follow
Toward your lake
Whose other side is light,

Whose depth
Drowns all swimmers.
And the women

Drift incessantly,
Burdened black
With narcissi,

Each less visible
Than a shadow
Among the many

Moving shades.

As One

As one who closes his hand on fog
And opens it to find it empty,

So I closed my eyes,
And when they were opened,
The colors had fled from my sight.

It was no use trying to remember the world
In its colors, the proper sizes of things,
Or the nature of my mission.

So I closed my eyes again,
And my hands also,
As a criminal who goes to his grave
Clutching his secrets,

When the strange animal asked,
What do you want, then? And I awakened

In a fright to a terrible chiming
Of clocks striking the hour

And the ravening colors,
And when I could not accept my punishment,
But still pleaded,

The tears began until
The mountains smoked,
And the sea hazy also,

And the fog rolled in, everywhere,
Even where
There was neither water nor rain.

V. FABLE

The Hovel

When the rich woman
Built a hovel

No one was surprised.
She had fed her Italian tables
To the termites.

She had smashed
The crystals of her great chandelier.
They were grateful:

They were so tired of glittering.
But pink roses came to visit her
Where she lived,

Arranging themselves in vases.
They would not be thrown out
But pressed their faces to windows.

When she tried
To pierce herself with their thorns
They pulled in,

And only later released themselves
Like the sly tongues of snakes.
In the night,

Silkworms wove curtains;
Grass covered her floors
Like velvet.

Night and day,
Four stars played on her roof,
Others flying inside

Or settling near her
Like lamps.

Children she never had seen
Came, calling her mother.
She was a pillar of hugs.

Her cheeks took on color
For children are rough;
A small white goat came;

A chipmunk brought nuts
And stroked her hand with his paw;

In rivers, fish pushed her to shore;
In fire, rain dressed her in its robes.

The last straw
Was the canary
Who flew in the window

Building his own cage of grass.
He was soon joined by others.

When she left,
She was crying.

The roses smiled,
And folded their tents.

Life would not leave her alone.

Whom

Whom do you love? asked the sparrow.
The rock, answered the lizard.
Although it is pitted,
It warms me,
And it warms to its core.

Whom do you love? asked the lizard.
Everything, the worm answered,
Everything

That can be taken down into the earth
And then resurrected,
And myself, and my magical doings.

Whom do you love? the worm asked the vulture.
Oh all the dead things,
And all the living
Who soon shall be dead things,

So sang the vulture,
Circling the worm who was tiring,
His mission almost ended,

And the trumpets blared and blasted,
And the sun pronounced saint on the vulture,
And the moon silvered the worm,
Making him holy,

And all were consumed by the long constriction,
The bottomless snake of the day.

Where

Where is the sun now?
Asleep in China,
On the great white wall,

Setting the temples to glitter,
Warming the fishermen
Setting out to sea in their small boats,

While the curried women stretch,
Cook their rice, yawning,
And the small children

Run through the streets
With their bookbags,
Their chatter filled with letters
We will never decipher.

And where is the moon now?
Wide awake in Egypt,
Silvering the pyramids,
That great snake, the Nile,

Speaking to the Pharaohs,
Who have waited all day,
Playful with the Sphinx's new riddles,
Teasing the ebonies of the ancient waters,

Netting the sacred cats in its haze.

And where is the rain now?
Traveling slowly
Over nameless, thick jungles

Where wild animals
Devour each other serenely
And herds of gazelles
Graze on wet fields of grass,
Dressed by a fresh rain.

And where is the snow now?
At the poles, at the cruel poles,
The two points of balance,
Where the earth turns over the sun

Like a wild boar on a spit.

The Raven Trees

In the raven trees
There is a stirring of wings.

There is a fluttering of blinks
In the raven trees.

There are green eyes clustering like grapes
In the raven trees.

There is a white frame house
And oh, it is proper.

There is an expanse of black grass
Between the house and the raven trees.

O lords and ladies,
Imagining cherubim
And tiny hearts,

Imagining hawks, vultures, crows;

Why can you meet only
When the white snow falls
On the black grass

Covering the black grass
The white house
The pale sun

The raven trees.

When I Spoke

When I spoke to the cows
They would not answer,
Neither the horses.

They changed their minds,
Speaking of the one day
They would no longer be dumb.

It was then that I realized
The sun and the moon had gone out,
A chill had set in,

My lips sealed,
Bones glacial.

Fable

How classical the elements
Of this scene,
Night rolling its dark carpets up,
Day arriving in its only way,

Breaking open like a bloom,
Transfusing the horizon with its blues,
The pink dyes fading,

And there it is, that scene from Aesop
(And every other fabulist),
The black and white cat crouched
Before the white barn door,

His whole body
A sun radiant with suspense,
And the unsuspecting, plain
Brown bird, at her crumbs.

Cat: Be not overly quick;
Use stealth, a bird in the hand;
Hunger makes for clumsiness . . .

Bird: Be not greedy, or the cat . . .
In the midst of every garden lurks . . .

The bird is safe in the tree. Composed,
The cat licks at her paw.
Laundry flies next door with awkward wings,
Spring's first true bloom.

Here, no one has ever seen
The cat catch the bird,
Or the dog the cat.

Yet there are bodies
Come upon suddenly, during long walks,
As if the blind feet knew the house of peace:

The mangled bird, still warm,
The cat, lying naturally,
But stiff,

In autumn, when the leaves
Blaze their funeral pyre,
In winter, when the snows prepare
The pure heaven of the woods,

Even in spring, as now,
With something to cover the victims,
Some of last year's leaves,
Dark dirt, rain-soft.

Not so in the garden,
Pruned and raked.
It is always in the garden
Death blooms best,

In that place of flowers
Where no hooves go,
That secure place with its tended paths.

In every garden, someone mourns,
While the wind rises,
And the laundry flaps, almost clatters now,

Like sticks farmers hang
To scare off the invisible, huge crows.

Digging the Earth

It was a strange day.
When she put on her dress
It ticked like a clock;

The clouds were sculptured
Of stone;
Later, she wondered—
Not fearing their fall.

All day long,
Faces floated over like flowers,
Although none of them spoke.

Soon, she claimed to remember
New York streets wide as Russia's,
The day starting up

Like an old horse
Pulling an ice cart,

A man in white
Sweeping his way.

She wondered at the light without sun
And the eyeless skaters
Dressed in black,
Gliding closer,

Trailing their long veils,
And their hats full of feathers;
Why she knew the name of the hotel
And remembered the kiosk in summer

When the lake lapped at the shore,
Odd things,
How in the heat,
Cement shone like snow;

Waiting for carriages;
Coal stoves before turnstiles.
There was something

About a bridge.
She wanted to tell them
About the store full of chocolates,
Its ceiling of angels,
Clerks at the counters solemn as tellers;

The great, disembodied arm
Under the tracks,
The staring bronze mask,
High as a house,

Prams, open trolleys,
Broken hearts
(Oh yes, that was a play).

Were you there?
She asked a face.
It cried and dabbed its eyes.

Her white lace hat
Dipped its flowers across her eyes;
She did not like

Its wide brim,
Nor its shadows.

She asked again.
There was no answer,
Only a sudden dark planet,

Nor would her fingers move,
Just the sun and the moon
Falling like stones
From her echoing rings.

And of course,
She had so much more to say.

VI. THE PICTURES

In the Used Clothes Shop

No stealing here, I tell you.
The hooks so high up,

It takes a stick to float them,
And roughly have they been pushed aside

To show the treasure,
The leather bag. Luggage.

In the picture,
It is the only gleaming thing,

And it seems painted with gold.

Three people stand in the shop.
The proprietress in her fancy dress
Scored with velvet,

A long white apron,
A hand dug into a hipbone;

She has parted her hair
In the middle

To show as much of her skull
As life will allow.
The rest is skewered into a rat.

Why is the lady with the small boy
Smiling at her, this gargoyle?

She holds a brown paper bag to her,
And her features have softened

Like a melon left too long.
What a treasure that bag must be!

She holds it over her stomach
Like an unborn baby.

And the little boy—
Why are children out of focus, always?

They are moving perpetually,
Whirling into position

Near one of those ladies,
Or one of those dresses or jackets

Skewered on hooks,
Used up,

At a touch, exhaling dust,
Their arms stirring, *use me:*

We are better than this woman says,
Who looks at this child as if to say,

A sad-looking suit, that,
I wouldn't give a cent.

And he is better,
Though under her gaze
He moves

And his face blurs
As if melted or smashed

Picture: In the Park

The photographer is all
Stiff black suit, stiff black hat;

He frets near the trees
Which live long, and without sorrows

And there he wheels up his shop.
It looks like a high chest,

On top, ten portraits, neatly displayed.
Oh the tree will lose its green leaves

To brown dust, but these photos remain,
Neatly displayed.

Not everyone wants immortality,
So he has a chair, collapsible.

He has his catch.
His wet plate moves

Toward the camera's maw.
Did anything ever look so black

As this picture of a man
Taking a picture?

The mother, nice in her little black cape,
And its nice white bow

And her black straw hat
Is already holding her pose.

She rests one palm on the pram.
The baby girl is straight

As a raised fork.
(Perhaps it is women:
They have this faith,
One picture giving birth to the other.)

She is all white ruffles,
Father, a black silhouette
Caught, staring into the cart mirror
For last, frantic changes

But left out somehow,
And as the shutter clicks

The child's face
Loses its faith;

She stares up at us patiently
With that gravedigger gaze,

"How could you do this to Maisie?"
But her pram wheels are locked.

The tripod
Is firm on hard rock.

How, Maisie, how?
And now we see, behind the pram,

An anonymous lounger;
He is all black,

He slumps black against a black tree;
He is set on spoiling the scene,

That random man,
And he does.

Bridal Picture

This is a wedding picture.
The party of six takes its place
In front of potted palms and palm fronds.

The bride is so overgrown by her gown
She looks like a child in its swaddlings.
Her headdress is a huge muffin cup.
Its veil is trimmed

With ribbons and tiny flowers
Sewn to look like a vine.
The dress has a tight waist
Wrapped firm in a ribbon.

Her face is round enough
To swallow her eyes, and her chipmunk
Cheeks puff out with marbles
Which will surely be children.

She wears stitched white gloves.
They emerge from the stiff
Starched cuffs of her sleeves.
Her sleeves puff out above them.
She looks ready as a surgeon.

Her husband appears to be the patient.
He can be identified
By his white carnation,
And how he stands, tilting away,

Creating a wedge of air between them,
But he has sneaked some fingers
Onto her right glove, and his hair

Is parted in the middle,
Combed into wings.

He stands with the expression
Of a long-distance runner
Waiting for the gun.

To the bride's left, and partly behind
Stands a young woman just like her.
Her arms rest on the shoulders
Of a seated man with a handle-bar moustache.
He sits in a chair of elaborate rattan.

His hands rest on his thighs jauntily
And he grins
As if he has just heard a good joke.

To the groom's right
Is a young lady resembling him;
She wears a white blouse, leg-o'-mutton sleeves,
An ivy corsage, a tight belt.
A white bow perches on her hair like a bird.

She has dark, onyx eyes.
She has one hand on her hip.
Her face is still, but her elbow
Expresses indignation at doings.
Her hair surrounds her face like smoke.

In front of her, in an all-white dress,
Is someone's mother.
There is only one mother present;
No fathers survive.

A stitched apron covers her white dress,
And its white streamers sail down.
She has a hand on her hip.

Her other hand rests in her lap
Holding lilies of the valley.

The white bow sits on her head
Like miniature horns.
She has a gentle, humorous mouth.
Behind her, the girl glowers.
She is probably her daughter.

The new husband looks ready to run.
The best man is about to laugh.
The woman behind him, who resembles the bride,
May be inspecting the photographer for dust.

The bride looks stuffed.
The groom has fine, sensitive eyes.
The indignant girl has two elbows that seem ready
To do quite a bit

But the bride and the girl behind her,
Who must certainly be her sister
Have the stone strength of dough.
As soon as they move

The young man on the right
Will burst into laughter.
The young lady with the elbow
Matching her eyes will turn to the others.

She will say something
And no one will forgive her.
They are already
Different as Union and Confederate.

And now the shutter snaps,
And now it begins.

Group Picture: The Family

1892

They are in the living room. It is some kind of occasion. A picture from the wall has been taken down and shoved onto the floor. Somehow, it nudges its way into sight. Have they just arrived and had no time to hang it? There is no happiness on their faces.

The three children sit before the oak organ, one on a claw-footed stool. They have put the blond girl, the oldest and tallest, in the center. She wears a plaid cotton dress, black stockings, and dark leather boots that button all the way up. They reach over her ankles. She holds her hands on her lap so stiffly, one hand forms a claw. Her dress is starched and her hands push the material over her stomach so it seems to bulge out. She is probably twelve. She leans so far to the left toward her small brother that the brother on her right, who is dark, seems to be sitting alone, though his knee and hers almost touch.

The small blond boy wears a wool suit and knickers. His shoes are like his sister's, his feet more narrow. The brother on the right sits on the arm of a square sofa with his legs spread apart. His suit copies his father's. His hair gleams flat with water. He stares into the camera as if he knows the pool in its eye will drown him eventually. They are all handsome children. They are all very pale.

The old man, their grandfather, sits on the chair, knees spread. He holds four fingers of one hand with the five of the other, as do the two boys. There is a checked cotton pillow behind him but he leans straight forward. At first he seems blind, eyes milky as plates. A closer look shows the light hitting his spectacles. They pinch onto his nose. His white beard is combed, although jagged, and his hair is quite long.

Behind him a blanket, rolled on a stick, is hung on the wall. Something bulges behind it. Probably the plaster has cracked and lets in the chill. In the picture, it seems without color, or else a dull gray.

The three children and the grandfather form a line going back into the picture, giving it the illusion of depth. A small panel of wall separates the old man from the father, who stands to one side of the rocker that holds his wife. His hand rests on the frame. They do not touch in the picture.

The father's head is not quite level with the painted tin tray that serves as a painting. A photograph of blurred faces, a hazy bouquet in a frame, nudges his elbow. In the picture, everything lives on top of everything else.

The father's head is square, and his ears stick out. His eyes seem fixed on a corner in the ceiling. His Adam's apple pushes out his collar like a cast-iron pipe. His watch chain loops out the other way from his father's. He wears a striped shirt. In the picture, all their clothing is dark. He stands with his back to the closed door. It is the whitest thing in the room.

His wife sits in the rocker, her back propped by a white pillow. She has the broad bones of an ancient animal skull, and in the picture, they are more striking than the flesh that covers them. Her eyes have slithered to the right like snakes. Her hair is thin and receding. What is left is parted in the middle and seems pulled back tight. She wears a print gingham dress that covers her entirely, even her shoes.

She seems to be mending something abnormally white. She has slid to the side of her chair for support. Her mouth is only a swelling. Her eyes seem to be forming a curse. Perhaps the material is only meant to cover her stomach.

The organ faces into the room at an angle, almost reaching the ceiling, curio shelf after curio shelf climbing up over the keyboard, demanding attention, a house in itself. Beneath its carved rim is a mirror. It is a gigantic doll's house in a tumbledown house. Sheet music spreads out on the carved rack, and the ivory teeth gleam like clean bone. It is clear it has just been polished. All of it shines like a mirror. It catches the light as if it were glass. A plant stand sidles up, offering begonias.

The brass claws of its stool shine like the sun. There are only planks on the floor. The wallpaper is so faded the picture hardly shows the design which seems to be some kind of emblem. The molding has a relief of wild ducks flying.

The six of them are arranged in a kind of V or the shape of a wishbone, the mother and father the short part. No one is moving, and no one is going to move. The doors will stay shut. The organ needs curios for its shelves. Instead, they have draped its carved top with feathers of peacocks.

The picture has opened a door that closed with the snap of the shutter. If the picture came to life there would be motion, scolding, cries, laughter, gray passion. On the back of the picture, *Amus hurly* is written in pencil. The hand is awkward and not used to holding it. In the picture, there are certainly sparks. We will never know if they mount to a fire.

Except for the organ, there is no beauty or grace. It is doubtful if anyone there knows how to play it. We will never know what lies in the stomach under the mending. Except for the peacocks, there would be no color and the peacocks are dead.

Lady at Night

The night is blue,
But everyone is smoking.

Screws of smoke keep rising
In the claustrophobic air.

The woman's face is huge and hard
As a stone puma.
Her thick lips are curved in a pout
Large enough to grow into a snarl.

She wears a dusky blue cloche
Pulled down over her ears, hard.
The hat matches her eyes.

Down its center slashes
A marquisette strip.
She wears the furrow of stars

Dividing her forehead
In negligence and contempt.
She is right for this place.

The slabs of cement rise behind her
And the tiny square windows
Glitter with the high polish of steel.

The street lights hang their gray heads.
Even metal sickens.
Behind that broad forehead

Rolls-Royces are stopping for street lights.
Policemen are going into dark buildings.
Glass cracks

Under someone's foot
And a dark woman startles.

This is an image of the twenties.
This is what happens
When the smoke swirls,

The sequins and rhinestones blink,
And go out
And everyone is laughing.

Let it be remembered
They always wore stars.
It was important to keep touch

With the sky.

Lady with Zebra

In life she judged too harshly,
Or could never decide at all.

For punishment,
She drove through eternity on a zebra.
How she came
To hate the sight of his stripes!

They drove over and over
A desert, yellow and infinite
And she was sure
She could count every grain.

She never got the same number twice.
After time turned immeasurable
She began to think

She heard grains of sand falling
And falling over an edge.
Her eyes swelled from the sun

And the gods gave her a veil.
Two spots on her cheeks
Baked like young apples.

Soon she looked innocent
As Snow White. She always rode sidesaddle.
The heat drove her quite crazy.

On the horizon,
Two giraffes watched her in amazement,
Stiller than trees.

She proclaimed them imaginary.
She was quite sure.
When a voice asked,

Nothing could shake her.
The next day, her zebra reared up,
And left her staring into the sun

Hearing the pouring of sand
Like a black waterfall,
Thunderous.

Woman on Peacock

This woman has gotten down from the moon
And right onto a peacock.
They have chosen

An electric-blue sky for their backdrop
And a landscape of rocks.
Nothing detracts.

Her dress is long and black
And her peacock is white,
A rarity himself.

The train of her dress
Tangles with the train of his tail.
Surprisingly, they never argue

Over whose is more splendid.
She has chosen a hat
Which wraps all her hair

And sweeping out from the turban
Two white antennas
Which curl at the ends.

God knows how she tamed
This miserable bird
Who eats flowers, bites ankles,

Or how
She has stopped him from squawking.
It seems done with mirrors.

She is holding one out to him
And they both see their faces.
O he is beautiful in his velvet choker

And pearl-drop earring.
(They choose to be viewed from the side.)
She has jeweled his mane

And stiffened it
So it rides like a crown.
He is pleased as a peacock.

What does he care about peahens?
Vanity is new to him.
What does she care about men?

The mirror's rays are needles,
Full of that drug, vanity.
They are lost in an ecstasy

Of themselves, themselves only.
The rest of the world is rock only,
Fool's gold.

He is tame and amazed as a puppy.
She is quite wild.
She knows

She will die on his back,
Holding the mirror

And is not afraid.
Because he cannot know this
He has no fear at all.

When her arm begins to stiffen,
That muscle, commonly called her heart,
Will begin its squeeze and contract.

The Vanity

Why did she buy this vanity?
After that,
There were always three of her,

And the mirrors exuded a gold light
And she was compelled to decorate
Their carved borders with peacocks,

To paint them on,
To drape them with feathers.
Life was always

In a rush in those mirrors.
Things flew by in a gold wind.
In the first mirror,

She is a medieval lady,
Watchful in profile,
Body tense, grown rich;

In the center,
She has draped herself
In a cape of cold silver,

Left hand touching her right cheek
(Is there a bruise?),
Right hand holding

To the jeweled robe of the lady.
Her lips are fuller, but whiter,
The weather

In this glass is colder.
Her eyes stare
And the pupils are wide and open

As iced-over ponds.
There are some gray feathers
Curling over her shoulder,

Nondescript,
Like gray leaves in dead winter.

In the last panel,
The moon is full and glares,
The clouds have paused,

She is in profile,
Both hands stiff at her sides
Her cape is all angles

Her pedestal, cold.
Stone is always
Cold to the touch.

She knows it;
Her expression is gentler.
She no longer minds

The staring eyes of the feathers.
She stares, too, now,
And she will,

For centuries.

VII. IN THE NIGHT

Emptiness

This emptiness is elaborate, ornate,
A design from an earlier time.

It took cunning to drape
The spaces,
Hold the voices back,

To move from one's place
In the earth.
First, limber fingers unbinding
The many tight strands
Of the vine:

The freedom of the bare arm—
Like a married woman,
In the marriage bed,
Divesting herself, all patience,
Of bracelet after bracelet.

The sun lights, but takes no space.
The trees surround in silence,
In uniform, both guard and gate,

Tapestries stitched
To existence, stitch by stitch,
So many variations on a theme,
The theme is lost.

And now
The mind opens out.
It is an archaeology,

The first day, common things,
Some pots, some pans,
One mug, a dish,

And then, deeper,
The flat stage, at last,
Curtainless, round,
Where dream after dream
Burned off.

And finally
When the wind
Blew through the skull
As it blew through the leaves,

A soft layer of loam,
And the one object,
Carefully packed against time:

There is nothing
Daily about it:

A form, a face, a rare note
Which is at once identifiable

By the song that it sings,
Scouring the mind
Of detailed place, recordable time.

Passages

Where in the world did the world go?
A hesitation at corners
For that face that seemed lost,
Then found,

A pause
To look into the snow-swirled
Globe of the old years,
The dated people,

Immune to the cold.
It was all

So innocent,
Just one more time
At the mirror,
A certain fear of strangers,

A desire for solitude,
Decisive, finally;
To be the lone tree
In the field,

Detesting even the shadows,
Those silent intruders,
And the uninvited flights of red birds,
Pausing.

When the rains stopped,
When the grass turned gold
(That deception)
Then brown,

The roots losing their grip,
Letting loose the stones
Held in their deep hands,

And life,
Whatever that was,
Going on,
Not pausing at all,

To the next field,
Crowded as any ark.

In the Night

That night,
The night picked me up in its arms.
It sang me every song it knew of.

It laid its cool blue body
Down against my hot one.
That was the first I knew the stars
Were all skulls,

Forever singing.
The moon rocked slowly back and forth,
Ticking in its chest.
I wanted to sleep forever.

The night sang the song
Of the falling leaves.
It denied the North Star.
It testified to the heat of the sun.

O lovely skulls, I sang,
Sing to me until the light comes.
They sang and sang
Until what birds were left

Lay down bashful and mute.
The coolness lifted from my skin.
There was no place to go but home.

The Gardener

Now the garden cries out with its many dry mouths,
And each leaf tongue accuses me.

I sit and am sullen, and something
Takes note of my ingratitude.

Soon it will tell me to count my blessings
And I will claim I have forgotten them all.

Then I will be reminded how my white walls sing,
And they do, for small birds

Have nested in them and hatched forth their young.
Then I will feel as the unborn

Who hear the world's strange music
Calling and calling,
And the music

Is blue and free
With neither cloud nor end.

Yes, I am already here with my shovel
And water, my pruning shears and my hands
Like a potter's.

The pigeons call to each other
And strut, and the air twitters like sparrows
But I crawl about the roots like any worm.

Should I have argued?
At times, rebellion is out of the question,
As are

Dramatic falls from one's heavens.
Conquered armies surrender, albeit with sighs.
Defeat is defeat.

As when, for example,
There is no denying

The white walls were singing;
The white walls are singing.

Postcards from the Country

I.
The leaves are thick, the trees gnarled,
And the children are always there.

The wooden gate swings open
And one child climbs on it.

Her big dog barks and upsets his cart.
The others run to right it.

The farm goes on, and the cows come home.
The brilliant light is gentled to shimmers,

And the steeple, comfortably remote.

II.
One man comes home in the autumn,
As the day drops, and the leaves darken,

And the blue pond grays.
He is prosperous, and holds his son,

While behind him, another
Wearily drags the oxen away.

It is the color of a storm.
It is only the coming of night.

III.
The ducks have gone, and the pond,
Frozen over. White as the snow is,

The mountains are gray,
And the sky, the water, all shadows.

The russet oxen appear like a sunset
And the woman, in her red wool hood.

The barn glows orange, as does the wet,
Newly sawed wood.

The weather pinches everyone's cheeks.
Truly, the people must be

The brightest things there are.